Cape Cod Visitor's Guide

Free and Inexpensive Things
To See and Do
In The
Lower Cape Area

Brewster, Harwich, Orleans, Chatham

William E. Peace

Cape Cod Visitor's Guide

Free And Inexpensive Things To See And Do

In The Lower Cape Area

Brewster, Harwich, Orleans, Chatham

ISBN-13: 978-1530521401

ISBN-10: 1530521408

Printed in the United States of America

Preface

Cape Cod, a tiny peninsula jutting out into the Atlantic, the "Outermost of Lands," as Henry Beston had called it, attracts over 5 million visitors a year. On a summer day, more than 125,000 vehicles cross the Sagamore and Bourne Bridges that span the gorgeous 7-mile Cape Cod Canal, and with that symbolic crossing, visitors often leave all their worries behind.

White-sand beaches, cranberry bogs, dunes, lighthouses, bike paths, gentle ocean breezes and plenty of sun are all here for all to enjoy, and easy to find! But there are so many hidden gems on Cape Cod, not exactly secret places, but places a little off-the-beaten path, that many visitors miss out on some of the best things to see and do on the Cape. And so many of them are free or very inexpensive!

And that is exactly why this book is written. It is written from an "insider's" view, by a local resident who knows all the ins and outs of Cape Cod, all the back roads, and all the things to see, with the intent of sharing some of these wonderful locations for more to enjoy. It is written with everyone in mind, from the children to the adults in the family! This book focuses just on the Lower Cape. From the Stony Brook Grist Mill to the Chatham Fish Pier, from the French Cable Museum, Jeremiah's Gutter to Nauset Beach, Bells Neck or the Three Harbors — there are many, many things to see and lots of "I didn't know that's" in Brewster, Harwich, Orleans and Chatham.

Take a little time during your vacation to see just two or three spots each day, maybe after the beach, or on a rainy day, and you are certain to reflect wistfully when you do cross back over that Canal. Each place that you visit will make you want to stay on Cape Cod even longer! Enjoy your vacation! Leave the "mainland" behind!

Stony Brook Grist Mill and Herring Run

A t Stony Brook Grist Mill and Herring Run, right on Stony Brook Road in Brewster, there is a beautiful mill pond and brook with inviting walkways all through the area. Everyone in the family will enjoy the visit here, as there are always many things to see. Stony Brook itself runs from behind the mill and then under the road, so you can explore it on both sides of the road. Three ponds provide the water to Stony Brook: Lower Millpond which we can see well behind the mill, then Upper Millpond and finally Walker's Pond,  both farther to the south. Starting from Walker's Pond, the water flows a total distance of about two miles, eventually crossing Route 6A just to the east of the Cape Cod Museum of Natural History, then continuing through the marsh there to the area near the end of Paine's Creek Road where the water enters the ocean.

A fascinating museum on the second floor of the grist mill includes a working loom with weaving demonstrations, often "hands-on" for children. The museum also has many photographs and displays that help us all to know more about the Brewster sea captains, the life in the 1800's, the many businesses that had been in this area over the years, and the native Americans that had lived here as well. The grinding operation of the mill is on the first floor, where you can easily see how the water moves the water wheel outdoors, then turns the gears that cause the top 1500-pound grinding stone to rotate and grind the corn into cornmeal. Volunteers demonstrate and explain the entire operation of the mill and how it works.

The herring run itself is best viewed from early to mid-April through May. On any one day, thousands of fish swim up the natural waterfalls of the brook as well as up the fish ladders, jumping several feet up in several spots, then resting in quieter pools just after a difficult jump. You will be amazed at the number of fish — you can't even begin to count them! The fish are actually alewife, and they breed in the fresh water ponds to the south and then return to the ocean each year to live and feed. The adults return to the ocean beginning in June, and the fingerlings return through the summer, so if you miss the actual herring run in May, you could watch for fish making the easier trip downstream. Once they are three or four years of age, then each spring the herring will swim back to the pond of their origin to breed there. The fish enter the brook at the ocean's edge, and then swim the entire distance to the ponds. Recent work at Paine's Creek has widened the entry way for the fish to improve their survival chances.

Another thing to see here is the huge number of seagulls which are incredibly clever and patient predators. It is fascinating to see how quickly a gull can swoop down and gobble up an entire fish. Nature is at work here, and holds many lessons for us about the struggle for existence and natural selection.

This area of Brewster was known as the Factory Village due to several businesses and mills in the area in the past. The mill that is presently on the site was built in 1873, replacing several mills that had been in the area starting with a grist mill

in 1663. That first mill had been located on the opposite side of the road from the present mill, down to the right. Thomas Prence had purchased the land at that time from the native American tribe, the Saquatuckets. Another mill, a fulling mill for making cloth, was built where the present mill is located, in the late 1660's, and operated until a fire destroyed it in 1760. A woolen mill was then built and operated at that location, too, from 1814 until 1871, first processing wool, then cotton, then paper. In 1830, a tannery was built on the other side of the road, preparing leather for use in the cobbler shop on Stony Brook Road, and for other uses as well. Both the tannery and the woolen mill were destroyed in another large fire in 1871; interestingly, the fire was caused by the miller smoking herring inside the mill. The current mill has been used as a grist mill, then as a clothing factory, then used in making ice cream, then used as a private residence. Finally, in 1940, the town of Brewster purchased the property and repaired the mill so that it worked once again as a display for the public.

You can walk around outside the mill at any time of the year, and enjoy the peaceful natural setting and reflect on what had been in this beautiful spot. If you wish to visit inside the mill, be sure to check their schedule at the Town of Brewster website; usually the mill is open only during the summer season, just on Saturdays for a few hours. There is no charge to visit the museum. Cornmeal is for sale during the summer as well, and the cornmeal comes with free recipes on the bag! In July, there is a "Mills and Gills" festival at the mill with many free activities, and Indian pudding to taste. In late August, there is an annual Cornbread Festival at the mill when you can sample cornbread made from the mill's cornmeal.

Directions: From Route 6 (Mid-Cape Hwy): Take exit 10 (Brewster/Harwich), and then follow Route 124 north toward Brewster. Turn left at the first traffic light, and proceed to the intersection with Route 6A. Turn left onto Route 6A and proceed approximately 1 mile to the blinking yellow light. Bear left at the blinking light onto Stony Brook Road. Parking for the Gristmill and Herring Run will be about 0.7 mile on your right.

Google Map QR Code:

About QR Codes:

Use a QR code reader app on your phone or tablet to scan the QR code here. It will immediately take you directly to a detailed Google driving map showing the Stony Brook Grist Mill's exact location. QR apps are free and easy to use and can be downloaded from Apple or GooglePlay. More information about QR codes is found on page 97.

Cape Cod Museum of Natural History, John Wing and Lee Baldwin Trails

The Cape Cod Museum of Natural History is conveniently located right on Route 6A in Brewster, and it makes for a great visit for the entire family. While this is a small museum, its two floors of exhibits and 400 acres of land are packed with fascinating information about the flora and fauna of Cape Cod. You can see exhibits about the whales, coastal erosion and the geology of Cape Cod, the life of the native Americans and of the settlers during the 18th century.

The Museum's numerous aquaria show many different species of fish, frogs, turtles, snakes, crustaceans, mollusks, and more. There is even a blue lobster to see, jellyfish up close, and many species of crabs! The museum also has three working beehives; one can be seen from inside the museum. There are many interactive displays and activities for children throughout the museum, so this is a place that they will really enjoy and remember. The Marsh Room provides a fantastic view of Paine's Creek Marsh and Wing's Island. Comfortable chairs and binoculars are available in the Marsh Room to use to view the birds and other wildlife in the area. An osprey nest can be viewed through the large Marsh Room windows or on a remote web camera mounted above the nest.

A favorite for many visitors is the 1.3-mile roundtrip John Wing Trail that leaves from the left of the building and heads toward the beach. It is a good idea to be sure to check the tides before going, as some areas along the trail can flood out during high tides. The trail winds through the woods to a wooden boardwalk over the open salt marsh. The trail then brings you to the beautiful 33-acre Wing's Island where you can view the coastal upland forested area.

From the upland area, the trail descends to the barrier beach, with views all along the bayside shore of Cape Cod. When the tide is low, the tidal flats and tide pools are an adventure in themselves. Here you can see many different fish, crabs, shellfish, seaweeds and all sorts of other living things. Wing's Island is an important historical location as well. Native Americans had settled in this area as far back as 9,000 years ago. In 1656, John Wing, a Quaker from nearby Sandwich, was the first English settler in this area (originally Harwich, now Brewster), building his home on Wing's Island; a marker there indicates the location of the original home. Salt hay was harvested from the marsh here for many years, and by the 1800's, the area was the home to several wind-powered salt works that evaporated the ocean water to produce salt.

Just across Route 6A from the Museum is the South Trail, also called the Lee Baldwin Trail. This 1-mile roundtrip trail brings you to a wonderful observation platform where you can see the Stony Brook marsh area. Stony Brook is an important herring run during the spring season, with fish heading south on the brook to the Millponds and to Walker's pond. Just past the marsh on the trail is an upland area where there is a beech forest. These beech trees produce a much deeper shade than

the typical Cape Cod pitch pine forests, and the forest makes for a memorable walk at any time of the year.

While there is an admission fee to the museum itself, it is a great place to spend a rainy afternoon, or even a sunny day! The grounds around the building are beautiful to explore themselves, with flowers, bird feeders to see, and picnic tables that can be used for a family picnic. The museum also has a gift store as well as a staffed library.

Directions: Take Route 6 to Exit 10, turning north on Route 124, taking that to Route 6A. At Route 6A, turn left (west). The museum is about 2 miles on the right, with small parking lots on both sides of the street. Parking is only for museum visitors and members. To walk on the trails without visiting the museum itself, anyone can park at the Drummer Boy Park just a few hundred yards farther west on Route 6A, but walking along Route 6A is not easy as there are no clear sidewalks there.

Google Map QR Code:

Drummer Boy Park & Higgins Windmill

The Higgins Windmill was originally built in 1795 right on Route 6A at Ellis Landing Road. The noise of the mill was a little too much for horses passing by, though, so the mill was moved away from the road; later, in 1890, the mill was moved to the Roland Nickerson estate, where it served as a golf course clubhouse for many years. In 1974, the mill was restored and moved to the current

location. The thirty-foot mill has a rotating turret attached to a long tail piece. The wagon wheel could be pulled along the ground to move the turret and face the vanes into the wind. Inside the mill, you can observe the wind shaft which connects to a large bull wheel with wood teeth. These in turn mesh with the pinion gear which connects with the drive shaft. This is attached to the upper 5-foot runner stone, which rotates and grinds the grain between the upper runner stone and the lower bedstone. Grain is fed through the hopper and shoe into the "eye" of the runner stone, an opening in the center.

On the hill next to the windmill, you can also see the Harris-Black house, a simple one room house built in 1795, originally on Red Top Road, and then relocated here in 1982. This is the only surviving house of this size from this period on Cape Cod. At one point, a poor blacksmith, his wife, and ten children had lived in this house! The house, which has a small loft, is a classic post and beam half-Cape in structure, with just 16 feet on a side.

Here, you can also see the Hopkins Blacksmith Shop here, originally built on Long Pond Road by Henry Hopkins in 1867; on Saturday afternoons during the summer, the forge is fired up and you can see a blacksmith at work making nails, hooks and garden and fireplace tools, some of which are for sale at the shop. The blacksmith shop had been moved in the 1970's to the old Fire Museum, now closed, and then in 2008 was moved here to Drummer Boy Park.

Adjacent to the windmill area is a 1-acre conservation land, Windmill Meadows, with a short mowed walking path amongst the wildflowers and birds. There are also several large glacial erratics, granite boulders left by the glacier thousands of years ago, with large one in particular that is called Whale Rock due to its shape. A wonderful playground is found at Drummer Boy Park also, with many play structures and a large wooden playhouse that children will love. There are picnic tables as well, providing for a perfect location for an evening picnic or just a place for parents to rest!

Drummer Boy Park is a fantastic, open spot, a perfect place to stroll and enjoy this peaceful location, perhaps even to fly a kite or play some games with the children! While the park is adjacent to Paine's Creek Marsh and the Cape Cod Bay, there is no direct water access from the park itself; the Wing Trail at the Cape Cod Museum of Natural History just down the road provides access to the Bay, however. But the large open fields and walking paths at Drummer Boy are a great place for everyone to enjoy a break from the beach. On weekends during the summer, there is an arts and crafts fair with many booths displaying all sorts of artwork. On Sunday evenings and on some special occasions, there is a concert at the bandstand, by the Brewster Band.

Directions: Take Route 6 to Exit 10, turning north on Route

124, taking that to Route 6A. At Route 6A, turn left (west). The Drummer Boy Park is about 2 miles on the right, about 0.1 mile past the Cape Cod Museum of Natural History, with ample parking.

Google Map QR Code:

R ight along Route 6A in Brewster, Nickerson State Park is a 1900-acre natural Cape Cod pine and oak woodland Park that provides many recreational opportunities from fresh-water swimming to running, biking, and kayaking, The Park is one of the most popular campgrounds in the state, with 418 campsites, many with water views, but Nickerson is also is a fantastic destination for a non-camping day trip as well. It is a wonderful place to spend a day away from the beaches and the crowds, and it offers many things to do. Everyone in the family will remember a day at Nickerson!

Nickerson State Park was originally part of the large land-holdings of Roland Nickerson. Nickerson's father had owned a distillery in Chicago and then had founded the First National Bank of Chicago. Roland had died in sorrow after the first home, built by his father for him, had burned in 1906. Shortly after his death, his wife Addie and his father built a large 16-room estate with fire-proof reinforced concrete and stucco. In 1934, Addie donated the land to the state in memory of her husband and their son Roland, who had died in the 1918 influenza epidemic. In 1935, roads and camping sites were built in the Park as part of the Civilian Conservation Corps projects. Many trees were planted as part of that project as well, including many white pines, spruces, and hemlocks that can be seen throughout the Park to this day. The mansion itself, which can still be seen on the north side of Route 6A, about 1 mile west of the Nickerson State Park entrance, was sold to the LaSallettes and used as a missionary from 1945-1980, at which time it was sold to the current owner, Ocean Edge Resort and Golf Club.

There are eight main fresh water ponds at Nickerson, and some smaller ponds as well. The main ponds are Cliff Pond at 0.7 miles across, Little Cliff Pond, Flax Pond, Higgins Pond, Ruth Pond, Keeler's Pond, and Eel and Triangle Ponds. For those interested in fresh-water fishing, Cliff, Flax, Little Cliff and Higgins Ponds are stocked with rainbow and brown trout each year by the Massachusetts Department of Fish and Game. The ponds at Nickerson are all kettle ponds, formed by enormous chunks of ice left in the glacial till by the Cape Cod lobe of the Wisconsin glacier nearly 25,000 years ago. As sand-ladened meltwater rushed around such blocks, small hills were formed, and we can still see these hills clearly in Nickerson Park. Kettle ponds are not fed by brooks or rivers, but instead depend on groundwater and precipitation for their water source.

There are wonderful hiking trails around Cliff Pond, Little Cliff Pond, and Flax Pond, and parking areas for these along Flax Pond Road, left from the main Park Road. Fresh water swimming is available at Cliff and Flax Ponds, with small sandy beaches. Just across Route 6A are the gorgeous Crosby Lane or Linnell Landing Beaches on Cape Cod Bay for ocean swimming, splendid sunset views, and tidal flat walks. In the Park, you can rent canoes, kayaks, and other small boats as a great way to enjoy the beautiful Park ponds. More than 8 miles of bicycle/hiking trails are also found in the Park, and the Park trails also connect near Route 6A to the Cape Cod Rail Trail which extends from Yarmouth to Wellfleet.

There is beautiful scenery everywhere you look at Nickerson, and a wide variety of tree species, including some white pines, hollies, cedars and spruce on some of the bike trails deep within the Park. You might see many different animals at Nickerson as well including fox, deer, and coyotes.

For visiting by the day, there is a daily parking fee during the summer and shoulder seasons. For camping, reservations can be made online at the Reserve America website; be sure to make reservations well in advance, though, as sites fill many months in advance.

Directions: Take Route 6 to exit 12 in Orleans, turn west off the ramp onto Route 6A toward Brewster. The Park entrance is about 2 miles on the left.

Google Map QR Code:

Brewster Tidal Flats

I f you are looking for a fantastic late afternoon activity, look no further than the white sands and warm wading waters on the Brewster Tidal Flats, one of the largest tidal flat areas in the U.S. Water can easily be up to 70 degrees or more in August and even higher in some of the tidal

pools. The flats are easily accessed from any of the Brewster beaches during low tide. As you arrive, be sure to first check out the beautiful and important dunes plants around the parking area: American beachgrass, seaside goldenrod, Dusty Miller, Rosa Rugosa (Beach Rose), Beach Peas, bayberry, Scrub Oak, Eastern Red Cedar, and Beach Plum.

During the low tide at the Brewster flats, you can walk out for hundreds of yards on the soft sand surface and enjoy the views, the water, the sky, and the many different animals that you might see as you wade through the small tidal pools. Just a few species that you could easily spot include: spider crabs, horseshoe crabs, hermit crabs, starfish, schools of mummichugs (minnows), sand shrimp, quahogs, clams, scallops, mussels, razor clams, periwinkles, whelks, and sea worms. You can also see many bird species using the area for rest and for feeding. It is a great place to just wander and enjoy; swimming, though, is best at high tide when the water is much deeper. Because the sun sets over the Cape Cod Bay, the sunset from the Brewster Tidal areas is not to be missed!

Currents from the west from along Sandy Neck and from the north from along Wellfleet bring lots of sediment into this area, and the tides themselves deposit material as well, resulting in these mud flats or tidal flats. On the south side of Cape Cod, the tidal variation is not quite as much, but on the north side, and in Brewster in particular, the variation is as much as ten feet, and combined with the buildup of sediments in the area, the result is a distance of many hundreds of yards between the low and high tide marks. Because this is the "intertidal" zone, the area is exposed to the open air twice each day. This creates a particularly harsh environment for the living things here due to the dramatic changes in water availability and temperature twice each day as the tide goes in and out. Most of the animals here hide in the mud sediments during low tide, but many are easy to see on the surface or just under the mud. Look for tracks from the moon snails, and air holes of the clams. This is a vital ecological area, providing food for many birds and fish in the water as well and also helping to prevent coastal erosion. Unfortunately, flats like these are at risk and need protection from pollutants and overuse.

Be mindful to time your visit carefully. You can park after 3 p.m. (check for any changes in that time at the beach gates) with no charge. However, you also need to gauge your visit with the tide; to spend an hour or two at the flats, it is best to arrive about an hour before low tide. Consult a tide chart for that information, and keep alert at all times so that you are not stranded far out on the flats by an incoming tide. The water levels will rise quickly. Also, be careful not to travel too far laterally on the beach; by doing so, you may cross a tidal creek inlet that is empty at the time that you cross it initially, and then full of swift moving and deep water, when you return. (I can speak from experience on this issue!). Only go out on the flats during the best weather. While this is a fantastic place for children that they will ask to visit again and again, be sure to stay with them at all times. Please note that no fires are allowed on public beaches, and dogs are not allowed on Brewster beaches during the summer. Shell fishing for soft shell clams, sea clams, mussels, quahogs, razor clams, sea worms or eels is only allowed by permits which can be obtained inexpensively at the Town Hall.

Directions: You can access the tidal flats in Brewster from any road leading from Route 6A in Brewster north to a beach parking area: Paine's Creek Road, Robbin's Hill Road, Breakwater Road, Point of Rocks Road, Ellis Landing Road, Linnell Landing Road, Crosby Lane. Park only in lots, not on the roads.

Google Map QR Code:

Punkhorn Parklands

T he Punkhorn Parklands is an area of over 800 acres of town-owned woodlands and kettle ponds easily accessible off Run Pond Road in Brewster. There are dozens of different trails that can be followed here, and a kiosk at the parking area provides maps and information about the area. Here you can choose a walk on a series of wide dirt roads, or can walk on woodland paths instead; both offer peace and quiet at any time of the year.

The woodlands at Punkhorn are typical of Cape Cod, with pitch pine and oaks the dominant species. But you can also see many other species including some beech trees and white pines with their finer needles. You might also find some blueberry bushes, and could easily spot some Lady's slippers or many other wildflowers along the roadways of the Parkland. Animals in the area include white tailed deer, red fox, coyotes, gray squirrels, chipmunks, raccoons, skunks, and more. A wide range of birds can be seen here as well. But the views of the many fine ponds in the Parklands are the special treat in this area.

A beautiful walk and a relatively short one, the Eagle Point Trail, just under a mile in length, leaves from the road just past the parking place. Walk on Run Pond Road a few hundred feet just past the parking lot until you reach the Water Treatment plant on your left. (There are several town water wells in the Punkhorn Park, and the area serves as an important watershed for the town of Brewster.) The Eagle Point trail leaves from the area to the right of the road and brings you past beautiful views of the Upper Millpond.

This pond is the largest pond in the Parklands. It provides the water for the Stony Brook grist mill about 1 mile to the north. In the spring, herring swim past the mill into the Lower Millpond and then into this pond and then eventually into Walker's Pond to the southwest. The view from Eagle Point, high above the water is a fantastic one, and there is a small bench there to rest and enjoy the view. Other trails that start at the parking lot include the Calf Field Pond Trail and the Seymour Pond Trail, each about 1.5 miles in length. As always on Cape Cod, be sure to stay on the trails to avoid ticks which are found throughout the Cape.

It is not entirely clear where the name "Punkhorn" came from. The area was described in a deed of 1747 as the "Sepunkhorn", which perhaps referred to an area of bogginess or spongy wood. We do know that the hills in the area were all formed by the glaciers thousands of years ago, and the ponds are all kettle ponds formed by huge blocks of ice embedded in the glacial debris. The native American Saquatucket tribe had lived here for many thousands of years before the English settlers arrived in the 1600's. They hunted and fished in this area, and walked on some of these very same paths. English settlers used the area for sheep and other farming as well as for timber, and eventually cranberry bogs were developed in the area.

There was even a small granite quarry here in the early 1900's.

Directions: Take Route 6 to Exit 10, turning north on Route 124, taking that to Route 6A. At Route 6A, turn left (west). Follow Route 6A for 1.2 miles and then bear left onto Stony Brook Road at the bend. Take Stony Brook Road 0.6 mile to Run Hill Road on the left, where, after a twisty and narrow 1.3 miles, there's small parking lot on the left for those visiting the Parklands.

Google Map QR Code:

Bell's Neck Conservation Area

A t Bell's Neck Conservation Area, there are more than 250 acres of forested woodlands around East and West Reservoir just south of Great Western Road in Harwich and along the Herring River salt marshes. There is also an area on the north side of Great Western Road, about 0.1 mile to the west, which extends into the upper stretches of Herring River and the marshlands that feed the river.

For thousands of years, the land had been used by the Saquatucket Native Americans, and then was purchased in 1668 by John Bell. Beginning in the 1960's, the land was purchased by the Harwich Conservation Trust to provide a peaceful natural area and to protect the important environments here. Herring River, which runs through the area, starts farther north at Hinkley Pond (across from Pleasant Lake Store on Route 124), winds eventually to West Reservoir, and then continues south from there past Route 28, past Lower County Road, and to Nantucket Sound. As the name suggests, this is a herring run in the spring, with fish swimming into the freshwater lakes to reproduce, then returning to the ocean later in the summer. The West Reservoir is man-made, created in 1925 by Marcus Urann, founder of Ocean Spray Cranberries, by damming the Herring River at Johnson's flume. Water was used to provide for cranberry bogs, several of which can still be seen on Depot Street. Indeed, East Reservoir was itself a cranberry bog until it was flooded in a hurricane.

From the small parking area on Bell's Neck Road, near the information kiosk, there are several options to view the area. Just across the road is the beautiful West Reservoir, a great place for kayaking or canoeing, or freshwater fishing. There are nearly always some kind of birds either feeding or resting here. Many other animals from rabbits to foxes to deer to coyotes live in the area as well. Trails lead through the woods along the north side of freshwater West Reservoir, and also behind the kiosk along the north side of the more brackish East Reservoir. You can also walk along the wider Bell's Neck

Road itself all the way to the bridge, past an old cranberry bog on the right. At the bridge, there are breathtaking views of the salt marsh and the river. Another dirt road, North Road, bears left off of Bell's Neck Road, and brings you to a small parking pull-off and a small pedestrian bridge where there are also fantastic views of the salt marshes and the river. This is really one of the finest views on Cape Cod, and a very quiet and relaxing spot.

A very nice walk leaves from Bell's Neck Road on the right, just past the old cranberry bogs on the right, but before you get to the bridge. There is a small pull-off area for cars there, and while the trail is not easy to locate at first, if you proceed up the slight hill to the left of the old bog, you will reach the wider trail. Staying straight on the trail will bring you along the southern shore of the West Reservoir, with some beautiful views. At the trail end, there is a herring fish ladder at John-

son's Flume, where the herring can be seen in April and May as they travel into the reservoir to breed. Here you can also see the dam that creates West Reservoir. On your return, take the path up to the right and this will bring you along beautiful views of the Herring River marshes, and then back to the original trail.

When you come out of Bell's Neck Road onto Great Western Road, you can turn left and then will find another small parking around about 0.1 miles on the right. The fine trails in this area bring you to the upper reaches of Herring River, and some very nice views of the marshlands that feed the River as well as beautiful woodlands. There are also close views of some active cranberry bogs, and while these are on private property themselves, they can be seen easily from the trail.

Directions: Take Route 6 to Exit 9A south. Follow Route 134 to the first light, and turn left there (at the Cumberland Farms) onto Theophilus Smith Road. Follow this 0.4 miles to Great Western Road, and turn left onto Great Western. Follow Great Western 2.1 miles to Bell's Neck Road on the right. There is a small parking area with a kiosk on the left just past the Cape Cod Rail Trail.

Google Map QR Code:

Brooks Academy & Cranberry Bogs

The beautiful Greek revival Brooks Academy was built in the 1844 by Sidney Brooks and was used as a private high school academy starting late that year. From 1880 until the mid 1900's, the building was first used as Harwich High School, then as an elementary school, then as a Town Hall annex, and then in 1988, it became a museum. It is a wonderful hidden-gem on Cape Cod, and a great place for a break from the beach.

There are numerous historical exhibits, but two key exhibits will interest children especially. Not to be missed is the working Harwich Railroad model which shows the railroad from Orleans to Harwich and includes scale models of the railroad stations and buildings along the way. Now, the Cape Cod Rail Trail provides a bike route along that same path. Another large room has many displays about how cranberries are grown, and includes many photos of cranberry harvesting and many fascinating pieces of equipment that were used in the past to harvest cranberries. The room is an excellent way to learn more about the importance of cranberry growing in the Harwich area. This has long been a key industry in Harwich, and hopefully someday there will be separate cranberry museum in the town.

Also on the grounds of the museum is the Anthony Elmer Crowell Barn. Crowell had worked carving birds in his workshop on Route 39 in East Harwich, starting in 1912. His world famous carvings are collector's items these days. There is also a Revolutionary War Powder House, which had been on the Brooks property, probably at Brooks Park just up Main Street, starting in 1770, and was used to store gunpowder and gunshot. There is also a replica of an outhouse; imagine walking a hundred yards or so away from the house on a cold winter morning!

There are also two memorials on the property, a Revolutionary War Memorial, and also a memorial to Jonathan Walker, born in Harwich in 1799. In 1844, Walker had assisted slaves in escaping from Florida to the West Indies. Caught by authorities, he was tried and imprisoned for being a "slave stealer." Federal authorities actually branded his hand with the letters "SS" as additional part of his punishment. Finally, there is a great gift shop to visit at the Museum with numerous books and Cape Cod souvenirs, and cranberry products as well.

Unfortunately for visitors, the cranberry bogs on Cape Cod are all on private property and not easy to see close up. However, there are several locations where you can get excellent close up views of the bogs, how they are built and how they work. One location is found by parking at the Cape Cod Rail Trail parking lot on Headwater Drive and walking about a quarter mile north on the bike path (stay on the path for viewing). (Take Route 124 north from Harwich Center, then take your first left after crossing Route 6, Headwater Drive; parking is 0.3 miles on the left.) A second location to see the bogs is in the Bells Neck Conservation area, on the north side of Great Western Road. (Stay on the conservation paths for viewing the bogs and do not enter the private property areas). You can also easily see the cranberry bogs from your car along Great Western Road between Harwich Center and Dennis, although there is no stopping and the road is a busy and well-travelled one.

Directions: Take Route 6 to Exit 10. Go South on Route 124 to the intersection of Route 124 and Route 39. Stay on Route 124 just past the white museum building and park on your right. Parking is behind the museum. There is a nominal charge for adults (over 18) to visit the museum, but you can get a pass for free admission just up Main Street at Brooks Free Library. Hours are limited, usually three afternoons a week, so be sure to check hours by calling the Museum at 508-432-8089.

Google Map QR Code:

Allen, Wychmere & Saquatucket Harbors

There are three harbors in Harwich Port: Allen Harbor, Wychmere Harbor, and Saquatucket Harbor. They are within a short distance of one another, and make for fine sightseeing for a sunny afternoon or evening.

Allen Harbor is named for John Allen who had owned property in the area along the present Lower County Road, beginning in the 1750's. The Harbor had originally been a salt pond with a small access to the ocean, and had been known as Oyster Pond and also as Gray's Pond. Native Americans had lived in this area for thousands of years before the English settlers, particularly in the area to the right (west) of the Harbor. Planting fields extended from the east shore of the Harbor to Wychmere. While parking is limited here, there are wonderful views of the boating activity in the Harbor. There is also a fine view from the bridge over Lower County Road, of the Harbor to the south and of the salt marshes along Doane's Creek to the north.

You can view postcard-perfect Wychmere Harbor from a small pull-off parking just to the east of Harwich Port Center. There is a fantastic, though steep, grassy area that is a perfect place for the family on a summer evening. Starting in the 1880's, the Sea View Hotel was located here until it burned in 1892. Originally, the Harbor was called Salt Water Pond. A half-mile horse race track around the entire pond was present here at the base of the grassy hill; it was a popular activity to watch the races from the Hotel. A similar track existed in the area just east of Trotting Park Road in West Dennis at that time as well.

In 1889, the town of Harwich constructed a channel from the southernmost part of the pond to the ocean, creating a small harbor. The harbor was named Wychmere, which means "salt lake," by real estate developers operating in the area in the 1920's. While there are no longer races to see, now, there is a beautiful and relaxing view from the pleasant hillside looking over the harbor at all times of the year. On the right (west) side of the Harbor is the Wychmere Harbor Beach Club, and on the left, accessible from Harbor Road, is the Town Pier which is used for commercial boats.

Saquatucket Harbor is named after the Saquatucket native Americans that had lived in this area. The harbor itself was built in the late 1960's by the U.S. Army Corps of Engineers by dredging the salt marshes along Andrew's River; a new board-walk, new harbormaster building and additional parking were added in 2018. The Andrews River still runs along the eastern side of the parking area and enters the Harbor from the northeast. A second brook, Carding Machine Brook, enters the Harbor on the northwestern side, just behind the restaurant. In 1820, a carding mill, operated by a water wheel, had existed here just to the north of the present Route 28. At Saquatucket, you can walk along the harborside and see recreational, fish-ing, and charter boats right up close. It is a busy and exciting area at any time of the day. Wonderful views and great food beckons at the restaurant, too.

Directions: Allen Harbor is on Lower County Road in Harwich Port. At the west end of Harwich Port, locate Lower County Road at the fork.Take Lower County Road 0.7 miles to Allen Harbor on the left. At the east end of Harwich Port, on Route 28, locate Bank Streeet. Wychmere Harbor is accessed at a small pull-off parking for 2 cars just 0.3 miles east of Bank Street on Route 28. Saquatucket Harbor is 0.6 miles east of Bank Street on Route 28, on the right side of Route 28.

Google Map QR Code:

Three Miles of Fun in West Harwich

In the short stretch of just over 3 miles from Dennis Port into Harwich Port, you will find a whole day or more of fun activities for the entire family and especially children. Pick and choose one or two activities from this stretch, and you will be sure to come back for more!

At the bend on Route 28 in Dennis Port, don't miss the Holiday Hill area! The Holiday Hill family-owned business has been a very popular ice cream spot for years, serving dozens of flavors of both hard and soft ice cream. Behind the ice cream stand itself is a bumper cars amusement area. In the bumper cars building there is also a great arcade with classic arcade games. To the left of the ice cream stand is a popular miniature golf course that everyone can play! And, for parents, there is a wood store that sells all sorts of wood products from picnic tables to shelves — it's a popular place to browse.

Proceeding on Route 28 to the east, just before you reach Dennis Port Center, you can turn right onto Hall Street; just a tenth of a mile on Hall Street will bring you to the Dennis Public Library, a perfect stop for the bibliophiles in the family, and then a little farther on Hall Street is the Mike Stacey Playground, a wonderful outdoor place for the children to play. Adjacent to the Dennis Port Village Green, the playground has many unique playthings on a wood shaving base. It is just a block from the shops of Dennis Port.

Continuing on Route 28 to the east, there is another miniature golf course on the left, just after you cross the Herring River into Harwich. A little farther east on Route 28, at the sharp bend, you will find an A&W Root Beer restaurant, a classic retro fast-food restaurant that is well worth a stop. On the other side of the road are trampolines that are a popular stop as well. A short distance farther on the left is the bumper boats, zip lines, and batting cages. This is a must stop for a hot afternoon, a great place to come right from the beach, and a great place to cool off. Everyone in the family can really enjoy the bumper boats the way that they have them set up. For the land-lubbers, there are batting cages that are lots of fun for all or you can just watch the bumper boats from the side or even try out the zip lines!

Finally, just another tenth of a mile on the left, you will reach the popular go-karts track. Sometimes there is a short line here, but the line moves quickly, and everyone in the family will enjoy the classic go-karts. For those not interested in the track itself, there is a fine antique store right next door! All in all, this stretch of just a few miles from Dennis Port to Harwich Port offers quite a few alternatives to the beach, and plenty of memories for all.

Directions: Take Route 6 to Exit 9A. Take Route 134 south all the way to Route 28, at the fourth set of lights. Take Route 28 to the left and proceed 0.7 miles to Holiday Hill on the left.

Google Map QR Code:

Main Street, Harwich Port

N amed after Harwich in Essex, England, Harwich Port has a long history of association with the nearby harbors and the ocean. Originally the area was where the Saquatucket Native American Tribe lived, fished and farmed. Beginning in the late 1600's, the area was settled by English settlers who soon turned to fishing and sailing for their own livelihoods. During the 1800's, several very large sea captain's homes were built along this stretch, and their beauty can still be seen. As time went on, several of the homes were converted to inns, and as the sea-faring declined due to the increased use of railroads, the area became a very popular resort destination on Cape Cod.

The Melrose Inn, just past Bank Street, was once one of the seven large inns in Harwich Port catering to the wealthiest of clienteles. The guests at the Melrose could enjoy sumptuous meals, clay tennis courts, a croquet court, horseback riding, fishing and sailing trips on Nantucket Sound, and of course the bustle of Harwich Port itself as well as the peace and beauty of the beach just a few minutes walk away. While the original building has been replaced, the beautiful grounds and architecture of the now independent living facility still attest to its glorious past.

There are excellent sidewalks on both sides of Main Street (Route 28) from Lower County to Bank Street, so Harwich Port is a great place for a family walk — nostalgic, picturesque and relaxing. Excellent parking is readily available in the municipal lot on the north side of the road.

There are numerous shops and restaurants along Route 28 in Harwich Port, and many art galleries as well. Clothing stores, bakeries, a jewelry store, a popular breakfast spot, a pizza house, and even a kite store round out the many different attractions here. Several banks and ATM's are right in Harwich Port as well. There is something for everyone to enjoy, but the biggest attraction here is just the stroll and the enjoyment of the summer atmosphere.

Arts and crafts fairs are often held at the intersection of

Lower County Road and Route 28 in the town park there. You may also enjoy a musical stroll night along Route 28, where local bands can be heard up and down Route 28 in Harwich Port (check with the Chamber of Commerce near the municipal parking for the schedule).

On Bank Street, it is just a short 0.3 mile through a beautiful tree-lined residential area to Bank Street Beach. It is a great walk in itself, or you could also drive down to the large parking lot there. A sticker is required for parking during the day there, but in the evening, it is still a great place for a short walk or swim. The water is warm in Nantucket sound, the waves are small, and the scenery is fantastic!

Directions: Main Street is Route 28 in Harwich Port. Parking is available at the municipal parking area on the north side of Main Street, right in the center of Harwich Port.

Google Map QR Code:

Playgrounds in the Lower Cape

Nearly every elementary school has a playground, but they differ quite a lot in just what types of play areas are available, the ease of parking, and so on. Some of the best playgrounds in the area can be found in the Lower Cape! Check out one each day and the kids will definitely ask to come back to Cape Cod!

Brewster - The Eddy Elementary school with a convenient location on Route 6A near Brewster center is one of the nicest playgrounds in the area. There are many different playing areas here and new playground equipment and surface. Basketball and playing court and playing fields, along with easy parking and plenty of seating for parents make this a great visit. Just a short distance away is the Stony Brook Elementary School, on Underpass Road. This is a great, modern playground right near the Cape Cod Rail Trail, with large playing fields and a large parking area.

Harwich - The Harwich Elementary School on School Street in Harwich is a very popular playground that encourages hide-and-seek type play. It is a wooden wonderland for children with many nooks and crannies to play, and is especially good with several children, but children will meet easily here, too. There is lots of seating for parents. In addition to the extensive play area, there is a standard swing set and a small traditional playground, basketball and playing courts and playing fields. Be sure to bring sunblock for parents as well as for the kids here. This is a great place for play at anytime of the day, or for a picnic, too.

Harwich - Brooks Park is a smaller playground, just a short distance from the Elementary School and just past the Brooks Library and Main Street, Harwich Center; it makes a convenient and fun playground visit. Several tennis courts, basketball courts, and playing fields are found here as well.

There is ample parking here, though seating for parents is limited. The area is located right on the Cape Cod Rail Trail Chatham extension, so it is a great beginning or end point for a short bike ride as well.

Orleans - There is a fantastic playground at the Orleans Elementary School on Eldredge Park Way, right off Route 6A near the Shaws Supermarket. This is a wonderful play area with a wood chip base. This is a new modern playground with many features including climbing areas, areas for tots 2-5 years of ages, as well as an area for older children. The music area is a special treat that the children will love. In addition to

the play area, there are large swings, and soccer fields, baseball diamonds, tennis courts and basketball courts. Plenty of parking and a shaded table and bench for parents make the visit a fun one for parents, too. Park past the school on the left, the playground is behind the school.

Chatham - The Veteran's Field Playground is located on Depot Street just a short distance from the Main Street of Chatham. The play area is right across from the Railroad Museum, so you might want to visit both in one stop. This is a great playground in a beautiful, open location. There are large playing fields near the playground, and tennis courts are near the museum. There are some shaded picnic tables for parents. Parking is limited, but well worth a visit when you are in Chatham.

Google Map QR Code:

Jeremiah's Gutter

Believe it or not, the first Cape Cod Canal was not the one that you crossed getting to the Cape! The first canal was actually in Orleans, and it came to be known as "Jeremiah's Gutter". When Henry Thoreau had visited the Cape in the 1850's he had remarked that it was difficult to get through the Orleans area due to the extent of the marshes there. Tidal areas on the east of Orleans would at very

high tides actually connect fully with the tidal areas to the west, where the Boat Meadow Marsh area is today. Indeed, early explorers had mistakenly thought that the outer Cape was a separate island.

As far back as 1717, the tidal creeks in the area had been widened by hand to allow for passage of small boats from Boat Meadow on the Cape Cod Bay side to Town Cove. The exact locations are now lost to history, but presumably, the canal did run near the present appropriately named Canal Road (there is a sign about the canal on Canal Road just across from exit to the busy Wendy's parking area)

and across what is now Route 6, probably through where the rotary is now, and then into Boat Meadow area. You can see some evidence of ditching still inside the rotary itself, with tall marsh plants testifying to that history. Evidence of the canal south of the rotary is long lost to retail parking and businesses, unfortunately.

The canal was built on land of Jeremiah Smith, and due to its shallow nature and little use, it was derisively called Jeremiah's Gutter by the local townspeople. Over the years, it was variously widened and abandoned. The key issue was that the canal, while it would shorten the journey around the Cape somewhat, would also bring the ship out near Monomoy Island, one of the most difficult and dangerous areas for ocean vessels. And on the Bay side, the tidal flats are not the deepest of waters, either. The canal was used, though, for some ships during the war of 1812. Late in the 1800's, the idea of the canal in Orleans was totally given up when plans for the current Cape Cod Canal took hold. In the 1950's, the construction of the Mid-Cape Highway obliterated most traces of the canal by filling in the area for the highway construction.

At the same time, there are some places along the Boat Meadow area where it is worth a stop to ponder just what might have been here in the past. One great place to view the Boat Meadow river itself, and a most probable place that the Gutter went through is right where the Cape Cod Rail Trail crosses the marsh. You can park at the small Cape Cod Rail Trail parking lot on Rock Harbor Road, and then walk about 0.3 miles north on the trail to see beautiful views of the marsh. The tidal inlet can be seen here to the north and west, connecting with the Bay. From the bike path, looking to the southeast, you can see the rotary area and the Mid-Cape Highway, if you follow the line of the tidal creek in a straight line. This, too, was probably the Canal at one time.

From the parking area, if you proceed west on Rock Harbor Road, you can then take Bridge Road, and about 0.9 mile north on Bridge Road, there is a fine outlook where you can see the ocean in the distance, and the much wider part of the tidal river here. Back on Rock Harbor Road, if you follow Rock Harbor back past the original parking area, and then straight ahead instead of entering the rotary, you will be, appropriately enough, on Smith Lane. This road turns left shortly and onto private property, but a small pull off is available where you can walk back along Smith and Rock Harbor Road to see the marsh and some of the inlets still there. There is also a nice conservation area with a walk that brings you into some upland woodlands looking down toward the marsh.

By going to view the present tidal system at these several locations here, you can begin to piece together the Canal that had been here so very long ago. It is a fascinating spot that most visitors to the Cape never see, never consider, and it is a fun adventure to step back in time, even with the sound of the highway so close. If Jeremiah only knew! Imagine if this had become the Cape Cod Canal, though, how the traffic would back up here on weekends getting over an "Orleans Bridge" instead of around the rotary!

Directions: From the Orleans rotary on Route 6, turn left onto Rock Harbor Road. The parking for the Rail Trail is just past the Court House on the right. Bridge Road is 0.2 miles further on Rock Harbor Road, on the right.

Google Map QR Code:

Rock Harbor

R ock Harbor in Orleans is a must see, especially at sunset; the view at sunset over Cape Cod Bay is one of the best on Cape Cod. This is a popular spot at any time of the year, and rightly so. There are always things to see here at the Harbor, from boats unloading their catches, to sport fishing charter boats and the hustle and bustle of the pier.

There is also excellent access to the beach itself and, if the tide is out, you can walk far out on the sandy tidal flats looking for hermit crabs, minnows, and many other animals in the tidal pools. This is an adventure in itself. Be sure to check the tides, though, before venturing too far out, as the tide comes in quickly when it does come back in. It is best to arrive about an hour or two before low tide, and then you will have time to walk on the flats. In the dunes area, be sure not to walk on or near the beachgrass plants (Ammophila breviligulata) - these plants helps to stabilize the dunes and protect the area from erosion.

Depending on the tide, you may see some trees placed to mark the narrow channel for the boats, these did not grow there, but were placed there intentionally. There are stories that clams fall from the trees, hence the trees are sometimes called "clam trees", but of course, those are just stories, although clams do abound in the area. The north side of Rock Harbor, which is actually in Eastham, is accessible from Dyer Prence Road, and is a great visit also, with a large parking lot and excellent views there as well. The harbor itself is a difficult one to maintain due to its location on the Bay; it is very expensive now to dredge the Harbor, but it must be dredged periodically, as it tends to fill in with sediment and organic material from the Bay. While there are more than 40 slips for recreational boats and 12 for commercial boats, boats can only get in and out about two and a half hours before and after high tide.

It is hard to believe that this beautiful harbor on the west side of Orleans was the site of a battle, but during the War of

1812, Cape Cod was not quite as peaceful a place as it is now. The battle between the British navy and the local Cape soldiers took place on December 19, 1814. When the war had been declared, many Cape sea captains did not support a fight with the British, as they feared loss of their important trade with Great Britain. At first, the British blockade did not affect Cape Cod's waters, but in May 1814, it was extended to include the Cape.

Rock Harbor at the time was an important packet landing for packet boats to Boston, and a harbor for other maritime trade as well, as many of the Cape ports were. The British Navy blockaded all of the Cape's ports, and periodically raided ships in port, burning them, capturing those aboard, and so on. They even came ashore, plundering homes and farms. Captain John Stuart, of HMS Newcastle, even demanded $1000 from the town of Orleans to not attack their saltworks and the town itself, but the townspeople refused. In Orleans, a militia was formed and the Rock Harbor area was guarded. Because the British ship was so large, it could not enter the harbor area itself, but barges of soldiers were sent ashore to attack the town; the locals resisted their attack successfully, though, and the British naval forces fled back to the ship. The ship then fired cannons at the town, but was too far offshore to reach anything. Eventually, the ship withdrew entirely and the fight was over; in just a few days, the war itself was over when the Treaty of Gent was signed.

Be sure to make Rock Harbor a stop during your visit. It is sure to be a place that you will remember!

Directions: You can access the southern side of Rock Harbor, which is the most "visited" side, by following Rock Harbor

Road all the way from Orleans Center. Continuing around the bend at the Harbor, you can follow Rock Harbor Road to Bridge Road and then left onto Dyer Prence Road, and this will bring you to the northern side of Rock Harbor.

Google Map QR Code:

I t is so easy now to communicate around the world, that we forget how different things were before the invention of radio. The first undersea cable to connect Europe and North America was laid between Ireland and Newfoundland in 1858. This allowed businesses and investors in London and New York to communicate. In 1869, a cable was laid from Brest in France directly to Saint Pierre Miquelon off the coast of Canada and another cable from there went to Duxbury, Massachusetts. Ten years later, the Duxbury route was abandoned and a new cable was installed from St. Pierre Miquelon to Nauset Light in Eastham. Why Cape Cod? It is directly on the route between Europe and New York City where many business messages were going.

By 1891, the cable was extended under Nauset inlet and to the office (also built in 1891) on Cove Road in Orleans; it was used for telegraph signals to Europe until the 1930's. In 1898, a second cable was set up directly from Orleans to France; from the station on Cove Road, the cable ran along Academy Road, then Tonset Road, Hopkins Lane, Champlain Road, and then under Nauset inlet to the ocean. A third cable ran from Orleans directly to New York City. The Orleans to France cable, called "Le Direct", was used for more than 60 years. Messages about World War I, about stock market investments, business transactions, about Charles Lindbergh's flight crossing the Atlantic all were sent via telegraph through this tiny Orleans office. Morse code was used to send the messages, and operators at both ends of the cable would read the messages and resend them on to their final destination.

The cable museum in Orleans has been restored to the exact way that it was in the 1950's when it was finally closed; by then, radio signals were in extensive use, and the telegraph had become a thing of the past. But we can visit the museum and see how important this telegraph technology was in its time, and how it worked. The museum is open with limited afternoon hours, posted outside the building, on Fridays-Sundays during the summer months. Tours are free, but donations are welcome. Guides will show you around the museum; some of them had actually worked in the station when it was active! You can see the cables themselves and how they were built to withstand the ocean. In the superintendent's office, you can see a map showing the locations of the cables, a small printing press, file cabinets, and so on, exactly as they were in the early 1900's.

In the operator's room, one of the cables comes right up from the basement, through the floor under the table. In this room, there are many different machines. One machine is the mirror galvanometer that used the cable signals to move a mirror, creating a moving light that could be translated to the letters of the message. The machine was so sensitive that when railroad cars dumped coal at Snow's which sold coal at the time, the vibrations prevented correct operation for several

minutes. (Snow's is now the department store on Main Street, and the railroad line is the bike trail that runs right next to Snow's. Just before Christmas each year, a large model train display can be seen at Snow's!) Another machine is the siphon recorder that used a small siphon-driven ink pen that was moved back and forth by the cable signals, resulting in a wavy tracing on a long, thin strip of paper. You can also see the automatic message sender that used holes punched in a paper strip to send a Morse code signal more quickly than could be done manually. The Kleinschmidt perforator was a typewriter-like device that could be used to efficiently make the paper strip itself.

In the test room, you can see some of the equipment used

to test the cables, locate breaks from a distance, and to be sure that they were conducting signals properly. There is also a repair room where repairs were made to any of the machines that had broken, Don't miss the basement! In it you can see the incredible support that was provided for the tables in the room just above, made of cement, lead, iron, and wood. Also, you can see the cables themselves. The cables are in pairs, one of the pair is the actual cable, the other is a grounding cable that extended several miles out along the first cable and then connected there to its outer coating. There are also batteries that were used as a backup power supply.

Be sure to take a ride down to the end of Cove Road, also. There is limited parking there, but the views of Town Cove are outstanding and not to be missed. It is a fantastic spot to reflect on the St. Pierre cable running through here, how some things change, and some things do not. Now we have millions of miles of fiber-optics cables that run below all of the oceans!

Directions: From Exit 12 in Orleans, proceed to Orleans Center, and turn right on Main Street at the gas station. Proceed on Main Street as far as the library, and then turn left onto Route 28. The museum is 0.1 mile farther, on the right, on the corner of Cove Road and Route 28. Turn onto Cove Road — the parking lot is very small, behind the Museum, and only for the museum visitors.

Google Map QR Code:

Nauset Beach

Nauset is a fantastic place for a long evening walk and to see nature at its best. You can of course enjoy the area in the daytime, too, as Nauset Beach is one of the most popular Cape beaches. But if you arrive about 6 p.m. you will not be charged  for parking and can enjoy several hours of incredible views. Nauset spit itself is a barrier beach that extends north to Nauset Marsh and south along Pleasant Bay to Chatham. From the beach parking area, you can walk about four miles to the south or three miles to the north. Low, irregular coastal dunes here protect the marsh areas behind the spit. Many plants help to maintain these dunes, in particular the American beachgrass; because of its essential role in controlling erosion, it is important never to walk through the dunes in areas that are not designated for walking.

As you walk, you cannot help but notice the enormous power of the surf here; indeed you will probably see many surfers in the water at this popular surfing location. You can also see how much the ocean changes the beach each day, and each year. During large northeast storms, strong winds drive the waves higher on the beach, and they often reach the base of the cliffs that you see here. As a result, the cliffs are eroded away each year. Recently, the restaurant and gazebo there had to be removed due to erosion; even the parking lot itself is now at risk. A very similar setup used to exist at Coast Guard Beach, with a parking lot of this same size, a full changing and restroom facility just as here, but everything was destroyed in a single storm in 1978, never to be replaced again. The ocean breached the dunes and its force could not be stopped. At Nauset, the shore is eroding back many feet each year. If you return in a year, you will notice the differences.

As you head down the beach, you may notice some large granite boulders here and there, these are glacial erratics that were dragged by the glacier some 20,000 years ago, and deposited in the glacial till here at that time. Some had been dragged from as far north as Maine and deposited here at that time. The sand here is gradually pushed by a process called longshore drift  from the Wellfleet area toward Monomoy to the south. The sand that you walk on here today in a few years could be part of Monomoy Island itself. The cliffs all along the coast are continually eroded away, and this provides the material to continue to move down the beach. It will take thousands of years, but ultimately, Cape Cod will be gone, eroded away by the forces of nature that here we can see so clearly.

The water here is very cold, as we are right on the open Atlantic here. This makes the area attractive to grey seals. The seals feed on fish just offshore, and if you walk south from the parking lot for a mile or so, you are very likely to see seals diving in the water and coming periodically to the surface for air. Very large colonies of seals are found on Monomoy Island to the south, but many seals do head up along Nauset as well. The seals are a key food source for the great white sharks, and you could spot a shark along here as well, they have been seen all along the coast here, although they do tend to congregate along the Chatham area. Indeed, the sharks have been spotted even in Cape Cod Bay. Of course, stay well away from any of the animals; while the seals are cute, you should not approach them, they are wild animals.

The waters offshore here have numerous shallow sandbars and strong currents and have always been very dangerous for maritime interests. When the Pilgrims arrived in this area in November of 1620, they at first turned south to head toward New York, but then they found the shoals here so bad that they turned north instead, and harbored just inside Cape Cod Bay, near Provincetown. Many boats have been wrecked in this treacherous area trying to get around the Cape from Boston to New York, and this is one reason that the Cape Cod Canal was built.

During the day in the summertime, Nauset has full beach facilities with lifeguards, outdoor showers, restroom and changing areas as well as a snack bar. Nauset Beach is a favorite place to watch the sunrise - if you are an early bird, this is the place, peaceful and yet with the constant reminder of the incredible power of the ocean. However you visit Nauset, it will be a visit that you will long remember, for sure!

Directions: To reach Nauset Beach, from the intersection of Route 28 and Main Street, Orleans, continue straight easterly on Main Street until you reach Beach Road. Follow Beach Road to its end at Nauset Beach.

Google Map QR Code:

Freshwater Swimming in Orleans and Pleasant Bay Views

A wonderful time can be had by spending an afternoon or evening exploring the area of South Orleans. There are several locations for gorgeous views, relaxing walks, or freshwater swimming. All the locals know these areas!

There are two freshwater lakes that are great for swimming in South Orleans: Pilgrim Lake and Crystal Lake. Pilgrim

Lake is a 39-acre lake with a maximum depth of about 28 feet. There is a large parking lot, and no fees. The small, sandy beach has both sunny as well as shaded sections. This is a popular and busy spot during the summer, but a great place for families to enjoy freshwater swimming and even a picnic at the picnic tables there. On the way to Pilgrim Lake, you can enjoy the beautiful views of Kescayo Gansett Pond on the left; there is a small town landing where you can find gorgeous scenery. Crystal Lake is another wonderful place to enjoy the fresh water for swimming, and perfect for families, too. There is a small parking lot for limited parking. The beach is a small, narrow strip of sand, but the calm, clear water and the beautiful views make for a refreshing alternative to the ocean beaches.

A wonderful access to views of Little Pleasant Bay is the Kent's Point Conservation Area. This is just a short distance back toward Main Street on Monument Street, from the lakes area. This is a dog-friendly walking area with access in several spots to the shores of Little Pleasant Bay, and gorgeous views along the way. Originally an estate property, this land has more than 27 acres bordering Little Pleasant  Bay, Frost Fish Creek, and Lonnie's Pond.

At the Packet Landing area, you can see beautiful views of Meeting House Pond to the left and Lucy Point directly across the inlet. This is a wonderful location to view boating in the area, as there is a marina on Meeting House Pond, and the inlet is the main route for the boats into Pleasant Bay to the right. During the 1800's, this was the main port for packet ships headed from Orleans to Rhode Island or to New York City.

Another great way to see the water views in South Orleans is the Paw Wah Pond Conservation Area. Here there are short trails through 12 acres of mixed forests of pitch pine and oak. The trails to the right lead along the marsh with pond views, while those on the left lead through the uplands. Both trails bring you to the shore of Little Pleasant Bay. Paw Wah is a salt pond, with the tidal flow bringing salt water in and out some each day. At the beach, you can walk the sand toward the pond and enjoy the views of the Bay, with Hog Island and Sampson Island just across the Bay. The Paw Wah property was bought in 1987 by the Town to avoid the property being subdivided into 7 house lots by a foreign investor.

Enjoy the South Orleans area, it boasts some of the finest hidden gems on the Cape!

Directions: To reach Paw Wah area, from the intersection of Route 28 and Main Street Orleans head south on Route 28 toward Chatham (1.7 miles). Turn left onto Namequoit Road and continue 1 mile to the small parking area. To reach Pilgrim lake, from the intersection of Route 28 and Main Street in Orleans, head south on Main Street 0.4 miles to Monument Street. Follow Monument Street about 0.9 miles to Herring Brook Way on the left. Parking is 0.5 miles farther, at the end of Herring Brook Way. Crystal Lake parking is on Monument Street, just past Herring Brook Way, on the right. To reach Kent's Point area, take Monument Street from Main Street and after 0.6 mile, turn left onto the unimproved road, Frost Fish Creek Road, and follow this to the parking area at the end. To reach the Packet Landing area, take Main Street past Monument Road, and then take the next right from Main Street, River Road. The landing area is at the end of River Road.

Google Map QR Code:

Jonathan Young Windmill

R ight at Town Cove Park, across from the Stop and Shop area, is the Jonathan Young Windmill. This is a fantastic place for taking those scenic vacation pictures! There is easy parking and a beautiful green with walkways down to the water and even a small picnic area with fine views of Town Cove. There is always some sort of boating activity to see here, and gentle breezes off the water will keep you cool on even the hottest of days. You can walk all around the mill, and when the mill is open (often during summer afternoons), you can go inside the mill and see how it is built.

Originally constructed in 1720, this 300-year-old mill is the oldest surviving mill in the U.S. Orleans itself had first been settled by English settlers from Plymouth Colony who were looking for better opportunities here on the Cape. The town of Orleans was given its French name in the late 1700's as a snub to the British who had attacked the area several times during the Revolution.

Mills were often built in such a way as to be fairly easily moved from place to place, and were often sold from one farm to another. They were an essential part of the communities at the time, usually grinding corn or wheat into flour that could be purchased at the mill. The strong winds on the Cape made for a perfect place to use windmills, and nearly every town had several mills.

The Jonathan Young mill had originally been constructed on Kenrick's Hill in South Orleans in the area behind the current South Orleans Post Office, and then in 1839, it was moved  to the hill where the Governor Prence Motel is now located. This hill was known as Young's Hill, and Jonathan Young was one of the owners of the mill at that time; it was right next to his general store at that location. Young was one of the wealthiest people in the town at the time, owned a large variety store and was the treasurer of the Cape Cod Railroad. Young had purchased the mill with several others, as an investment. In 1897, he sold the mill to Henry Hunt; the mill was transported down to the water's edge by oxen, then barged all the way to Hyannis Harbor, and then up to Scudder Ave. in Hyannisport by oxen again, where it was used on and off until 1983. At that time, it was moved, in over 1000 pieces, to its present location where it was reassembled and restored.

Originally there were at least four different windmills in Orleans, but over the years, they were all lost or moved to other locations. While the Jonathan Young mill no longer grinds grain, it could, as it has all interior parts still intact, just as they were in the 1700's. The mill, like many mills built in that period, has a rotating cap that can be moved to face into the wind by using the tailpiece attached to the wheel. The wind vanes turn the wind shaft which connects with wood gears to a vertical drive shaft which is connected to the top grinding stone, turning it on top of the lower stone, with the grain fed into the space between the two stones. Much of the machinery inside the mill is the original work.

Directions: Take Rt. 6, to the Orleans Rotary. Exit the rotary onto Rt. 28 toward Orleans and Chatham. Turn left at the first set of lights, across from the Stop and Shop area, into the Windmill parking area.

Google Map QR Code:

Chatham Fish Pier

A fantastic place for enjoying refreshing ocean breezes, beautiful ocean scenery, lots of things to see, and wonderful food is the Chatham Fish Pier. There is an excellent observation platform above the pier that allows you to look down on the fishing fleet operations and get some memorable pictures. This area, along with other piers that have come and gone over the years, has been an important location for fishing operations since the 1700's. The fish pier was built by the town of Chatham in 1946, and updated in 1980 and 2019.

You can see fishing boats coming and going here with crabs, scallops, lobsters, skate, dogfish, halibut, pollock, flounder, haddock, swordfish, cod and many more types of seafood. Pier Host volunteers, most of whom had been commercial fishermen themselves, are often at the pier to explain just what it is that is going on and what kinds of fish are being loaded. They can share tales of their own fishing experiences, and tell you about the changes over time of the different types of fish being caught.

Many of the fishing boats are family operations, run by just two or three family members. Just under a hundred boats operate out of Chatham Harbor. They usually leave before dawn, so to see them heading out for the day, you would need to start your own day quite early. They may go out anywhere from 3 to 125 miles or so, depending on the type of fishing that they are doing. Many of them return  anywhere from ten or so to three, depending on just how far out they had been fishing, so that is the best time of day to watch them as they come in to the pier. At the pier, the fish is placed into a large metal conveyer bucket, then dumped through a chute into the packing room where it is placed on more ice and sent by truck to local stores and restaurants or to fish markets in Boston, New York or New Bedford.

There is a restaurant right at the fish pier where you can buy some of the freshest fish in New England, nearly right off the boat. You can buy many different seafoods from lobster to fish and chips to clam chowder, or you can buy seafood to take home to cook on your own. Near the pier, you can also see a monument to the fishing industry. The monument, named "The Provider," was built in 1992 to honor the hard work of the fisherman here in Chatham.

Most likely you will also see many seagulls and seals at the harbor as well. Kids will love watching the seals and the gulls; just the interactions of the gulls and seals is quite interesting to see! While the best place to see the seals is down along Monomoy Island itself, many seagulls and seals do come up this way looking for pieces of fish that have been dropped or discarded.

The view from the pier is a stunning and relaxing one, of Aunt Lydia's Cove. Tern Island is to your left; it is an Audubon wildlife sanctuary. Far to the right and over the Chatham Inner Harbor waters are the sandbars of Chatham, known as the Chatham Bars. This has always been a difficult area for maritime navigation, and one that has caused many boating accidents over the years. We really do learn to appreciate the hard work of the Chatham fishermen with a short visit to the Chatham Fish Pier.

Directions: The Chatham Fish Pier is located right on Shore Road. Park in the upper lot and walk down the hill, following the safety lines to the pier and observation deck there.

Google Map QR Code:

Chatham Railroad Museum

I n the early 1850's, the Cape Cod Branch Railroad began to extend lines from mainland Massachusetts onto Cape Cod and by 1854, had reached Hyannis. In 1865, the Cape Cod Central Railroad had opened a line from Yarmouth to Orleans, along the current Cape Cod Rail Trail. All of these lines subsequently became part of the Old Colony Railroad which operated in much of eastern Massachusetts and Rhode Island.

The 7 mile service from Harwich to Chatham, along the route of what is now a spur of the Cape Cod Rail Trail, began in 1887. The beautiful Victorian Railroad Gothic style railroad station on Depot Street in Chatham opened that same year, and it now serves as the Chatham Railroad Museum. At one point, more than 20,000 people rode the line each year and the Chatham station had a repair shop for trains, fuel storage, and a turntable to rotate the train cars back toward Harwich.

The railroad ran four passenger trains daily as well as freight trains that carried out Cape Cod products from cranberries to fish, and brought in products such as lumber, wiring, and fuel, all being used in the growing Cape economy of the time. Service to Chatham ended in 1937, the tracks were abandoned and the path was unused until the recent extension of the Cape Cod Rail Trail from the bike rotary in Harwich to Crowell Road in Chatham, just a block from the museum. The station itself was also abandoned, then purchased in 1951 by Mrs. Jacob Cox who subsequently donated it to the Town of Chatham.

The museum is an ever-popular attraction for children and for their parents alike, and there is no admission fee (donations welcome); hours may change but recently were from 10-4 from Tuesday through Saturday during the summer months. Many artifacts about railroading are found here including a caboose on railroad tracks that children can climb right into. The fully-restored wooden red caboose was built in 1910 by the New York Central Railroad, and was used on freight trains that ran from Chicago to New York City.

Lanterns, tools, working Western Union telegraph equipment, railroading signs and timetables are all on display inside the museum. Children can play at the ticket booth, making believe that they are buying or selling tickets; it is a perfect spot for many photo opportunities! The booth is set up just as it was when the station was in operation. In what was once the waiting room of the station, you will find many train models, badges, calendars, photographs, documents, and fascinating displays of all sorts related to railroads. There is  also a scale-model diorama showing the Chatham Railroad Yard in 1915 as well as NY Central locomotive models that were used in the 1939 NY World's Fair. Friendly and knowledgeable volunteers will answer any questions that you have, and have many stories to tell! This is a fun, kid-friendly museum, and just across the street there is a great playground!

Directions: Take Route 28 from Harwich to the rotary just before Chatham Center. At the rotary, bear left, staying on Route 28. Depot Road is one block on the left. The museum itself is just 0.1 mile on the right. Parking is limited.

Google Map QR Code:

Benjamin Godfrey Windmill & Chase Park

T he Benjamin Godfrey windmill was built just after the American Revolution, in 1797; it was originally situated on the hill just to the east of Stage Harbor. Godfrey was a prominent citizen in Chatham, and had led the local militia to the Boston Battle of Bunker Hill in 1775, during the Revolution. During the 1800's, the mill, like many Cape Cod mills, was owned by several different owners and used most of the time to produce ground cornmeal and flour for local use.

In the 1800's, there were as many as eleven different windmills operating in Chatham alone. During the early 1900's, many severe storms caused serious damage to the

Godfrey mill, unfortunately. At one point, the mill was sold for just $575. In 1939, the mill was moved to a location near Mill Pond, and then in 1956, the mill was acquired by the Town of Chatham. At that time, it was moved to its present location at Chase Park, but the mill did come into disrepair over time.

The mill is 30 feet tall and 22 feet in diameter, with three stories inside, and that made it the tallest windmill on the Cape. Notice that there are two doors on opposite sides; this was to make it safer to enter or leave the mill — the moving vanes could kill a person or animal. The vane and the flax or cotton sails that turn the mill are attached to the windshaft on one side, and a 37-foot tail piece is attached on the other side and also to a wheel on the ground. The tail piece could be moved by several people or using a horse to rotate the vanes into the wind. The best windspeeds were about 10-25 mph.

Inside, the windshaft connects to a vertical shaft through a set of wooden gears. The vertical drive shaft turns the upper granite millstone, with the grain being fed through a hopper and an opening in the top millstone into the space between the two stones. The ground grain falls from the edge of the stones through chutes and down to the lower level where the grain was bagged for sale. Corn was frequently ground in this grist mill to make cornmeal, and wheat and rye were also ground, to produce whole wheat or white flour.

The eight-sided wind mill was just recently renovated in 2012. Extensive reconstruction work was done including re-building the first floor, replacing the wind vanes, the wind-shaft, and the exterior cedar shingling. The swordfish weathervane was added at that time as well. Just in time for the tricentennial of the Town in 2012, the mill was fully restored and able to function fully as a grist mill once again.

The mill is open for viewing during limited hours, often during early afternoons on Mondays, Wednesdays and Fridays during the summer months. The mill is not in use at all times, but you can get inside at these times to see the inner workings of the mill. Usually during one Saturday in June and one in August, the mill is used to grind corn and then you can purchase the cornmeal. This coincides with the Chatham History Weekend and the Chatham Festival of the Arts.

While you are at the mill, you can enjoy the very pleasant Chase Park. It is a perfect place for a picnic, with several picnic tables, charcoal grills, and restrooms. Behind the windmill you will find the Chatham Labyrinth, definitely a fun time for all. This labyrinth is based on an ancient design, and is intended as a place for quiet, meditative thinking and personal reflection. It is said that by following the path to the center, we reach a relaxed state of wholeness. There are benches to the side of the labyrinth, too, for onlookers. There are also two playing courts that can be used for bocce or petanque.

Directions: Take Route 28 from Harwich into the Chatham area. At the Chatham rotary, turn right onto Stage Harbor Road. Follow this 0.4 miles to Cross Street on the left. Follow this 0.3 miles to Shattuck Place on the right. Follow Shattuck Place 0.2 miles to the small parking area for the park and windmill.

Google Map QR Code:

Chatham Lighthouse

A visit to the lower Cape is not complete without a visit to the Chatham Light area. This area is popular at all times of the day, and the view cannot be rivalled. Here you can look out over the Nauset Spit, Chatham Bars and North Monomoy Island. Bincoculars are available and are great for spotting seals in the water or on the sands. The beach is Chatham's most popular beach, Lighthouse Beach, and makes for a wonderful evening walk.

The bars are shallow shoals that have over the years been a treacherous place for navigators. Indeed, when the Pilgrims first saw land just to the north of here, they were planning on sailing south around the elbow of the Cape and then onto New York. They sailed along this area, but then decided it would be more prudent to head north and then into the calmer Cape Cod Bay. Were it not for these shoals, and swift currents offshore, history may have turned out very differently than it did. The inlet through Nauset spit, right in front of the observation area, was formed during a strong northeast storm in 1987. To the left is the area of Chatham Harbor, the Fish Pier is just 1.3

miles to the left on Shore Road. To the right of the observation area is North Monomoy Island. The area is named for the Monomoy native Americans that had lived here for thousands of years before the English settlers arrived. The local school district is the Monomoy Regional District.

Chatham Light is the second lighthouse to be built on Cape Cod. (Highland Light in Truro was the first.) The lighthouse was built in 1808, on Jame's Bluff that looks out over Chatham Bars and the open Atlantic. The idea was to provide a second key lighthouse along the treacherous outer Cape area. In order to distinguish the location from the single Highland Lighthouse, two matching towers were built here in Chatham; they were known as the "Twin Lights". One tower was actually moveable so that they could be lined up with the available passageway through the Chatham bars. The forty-foot towers were built of wood and each included six lights with silver-coated reflectors.

By 1841, though, the towers had deteriorated and were replaced with brick towers at that time. Then, by 1879, both of those towers had tumbled into the ocean due to the continuing erosion of the cliff here. Two new 80 foot lighthouses were built at that time (1877), fueled first using lard oil and then kerosene. The towers were made of cast iron, and lined with brick. In 1923, the northernmost of the two towers was removed and taken 12 miles north to Nauset Beach to become Nauset Light — it is still there today.

The southernmost tower remains in Chatham today just to the left of the original lighthouse keeper's house, which now serves as a Coast Guard Station. The concrete foundation area from the northernmost light can still be seen to the immediate right of the Coast Guard building. In 1939, the lighthouse was electrified with a 1000-watt bulb and an electric motor. In 1969, the entire lighthouse top (lantern) was rebuilt and aerobeacons were installed to replace the light and Fresnel lens system. The original lens is still on display at the Atwood House in Chatham. The lighthouse was automated in 1982 and is still an important navigation light on Cape Cod.

The lighthouse can be toured on summer Wednesdays for several hours; the Chatham Chamber of Commerce on Main Street right in town can provide specific hours, which are subject to change.

Directions: Take Route 28 from Harwich to the rotary in Chatham. Then continue straight through the center of town on Main Street. After the center of town, turn right, still on Main Street, and follow this to Chatham Lighthouse on the right. Short term parking is on the other side of the road.

Google Map QR Code:

Main Street, Chatham

C hatham is a scenic, pleasant Cape Cod village at the very elbow of Cape Cod. With the open Atlantic to the east and Nantucket Sound to the south, Chatham has a particularly comfortable climate in the summer; there is always a breeze in the evening and this, and the many things to see and do here make Chatham's Main Street a great place to spend an afternoon or evening browsing. There are many different shops along Main Street; you can find just about anything that you want here from Cape Cod T-shirts to fine jewelry. Main Street is a fun stroll with sidewalks along both sides of the street, and several parking areas behind the store buildings. Many people make a visit to Main Street in Chatham a part of their vacation every year.

There are numerous clothing stores, consignment stores, several bookstores, a general store, and several gift and toy stores. There is even an old fashioned "five and ten" store. There are many art galleries along Main Street, also, with photographs, paintings, sculpture, pottery, jewelry and many other types of art of display by local artists. Several antique shops are found on Main Street, too. You will find candy,

 fudge, ice cream, full restaurant fare, and casual restaurants as well. There are so many very popular restaurants along Main Street that is is hard to keep count! People come from quite far just to come to some of these restaurants for a great Cape Cod meal!

Main Street has no parking meters, but parking can be tight in the summer either on the street or in the lots behind the stores. During the summer, this is a very busy pedestrian area, and Main Street is very narrow, so be particularly careful driving, even in opening your doors! If you park on the street, be absolutely certain to be correctly parked or you may be ticketed. There are several parking places including: Colonial Building lot (from the Rotary, take Stage Harbor Road, then turn left into the lot (after the bank lot); Town Hall lot (right off of Main Street, just to the east of the Town Hall); and Chatham Bars Avenue lot (turn north from Main Street onto Chatham Bars Avenue, parking is on the left). Several stores also have small private parking areas for their customers, just behind their stores.

The main business area of Main Street itself is less than a mile long, but if you continue your walk or drive to the east about a mile, you will eventually reach the beautiful overlook at Chatham Lighthouse. If you visit Main Street, don't miss the Chatham Light area!

After your shopping, each week there is a free band concert by the all-volunteer Chatham Band. People come from all around to attend these excellent concerts! Concerts, about an hour and a half in length, usually being right around 8 in the evening on Fridays during July and August. Many people bring blankets (it can be cool), chairs, and even a picnic dinner to enjoy during the concert. The concerts are at the Town Bandstand, located in Kate Gould Park on Chatham Bars Avenue. Parking at the Park is only for band members, so you need to park elsewhere for the concert.

Another "after shopping" option is Veterans Field, just behind the Recreation Center (just west of the rotary). This is a great spot to watch a Cape Cod Baseball League game in the early evening. Many of these players become professional players. There is a nice playground there, too, if the children have lost some of their enthusiasm about the shops on Main Street!

Directions: Take Route 28 from Harwich to the Chatham Rotary. Main Street in Chatham is just to the east and west of the rotary itself.

Google Map QR Code:

Monomoy National Wildlife Refuge

The Monomoy National Wildlife Refuge offers gorgeous views and walking trails that take you along the south coast of Chatham to Morris Island, with views of the beautiful dunes-covered barrier islands, North  Monomoy and South Monomoy Island that stretch some 8 miles south of Chatham Harbor. Here, the sands are moving south with each tide, gradually lengthening Monomoy. Periodically, storms overwash parts of the islands, then more sand drifts down from the north again, resulting in a continually changing landscape.

The area is a critical one as an important habitat for migratory birds that stop here to feed, rest, or nest. Piping plovers, roseate terns, common terns, oystercatchers and hundreds of other species make their homes here at one time or another during the year. Many research projects are underway each year in the Refuge, and each summer interns work here helping visitors and conducting research. The islands are also home to one of the largest gray seal populations in the U.S. Most of the seals are on the Atlantic Ocean side of the Monomoy Islands, but you may see some seals along Morris Island. (You can also see seals at the Chatham Fish Pier and at Nauset Beach). Great white sharks have also been attracted to the seal population as a food source, so it is entirely possible to view a great white in this area, although this is most likely closer to the seal population.

Access to the islands themselves is possible by boat. The island is 8 miles long and tides and changes due to storms can cause huge difficulties, so be certain to stop at the Refuge Visitor Center to discuss your plans. There are several different private tours available from Chatham or Harwich areas. But you can experience some of the beauty of Monomoy by walking on the shorter trails from the Refuge headquarters to Morris Island. Indeed, in 1944 when the Refuge was established, Morris Island and Monomoy Island were joined, later to be separated by storms. Trail maps available at the Visitor Center will guide you through the beautiful sights that you will see along these ¾ mile trails. Part of the trail goes along the shore, down to the left of the weather dome building, so it is important to walk when tide is going out.

Arrive about 2 hours before low tide. It is possible to walk on the private roads to get access to the island, or to get back from the island, but there is no parking at all past the visitor center, so don't even try! Again, it is best to stop at the visitor center first to discuss your plans. The ocean is not forgiving of mistakes. At the visitor center, which is open during the summer season, you can also see many exhibits about the wildlife here, displays of how Monomoy has changed over time, an outdoor garden, and even some games for the children! They also have specific guidelines for visitors in the Refuge: in general, take nothing at all except for photographs, and leave only footprints! Restroom facilities are available at the visitor center as well.

Just to the left of the visitor center is the radiosonde monitoring dome and in the building beneath the dome, the Morris Island Upper Air work area where weather balloons are prepared for launch. Two National Oceanic and Atmospheric Administration (NOAA) balloons are launched daily, at about 7 AM and 7 PM. The natural latex balloons are filled with helium until they are about 5 feet in diameter; this process takes about 7-10 minutes alone. Then an orange parachute is attached, and a battery-powered radiosonde. The radiosonde monitors temperature, humidity and pressure and transmits the information back to the station here in Chatham. From there, the information is combined with data from more than 100 other balloons released in the U.S. at the same time, providing significant information for weather forecast computer models about conditions in the atmosphere, and aiding enormously in the weather forecasts and predictions of severe weather conditions that the National Weather Service can provide. As the balloon rises, the pressure around it grows lower, causing the balloon itself to expand in size until it is about the size of a house! Eventually, at about 20 miles high, it bursts, and the radiosonde falls back to earth. Typically, the device is in the air for about 2 hours before the balloon bursts, and it travels up to several hundred miles. A note on the device asks that it be returned to NOAA, although only about 20% ever get back to NOAA. You are welcome to watch the launch process and ask questions if you are there at the right time. It is a fascinating time for all!

Over the years, Monomoy area has had a fascinating history. For thousands of years, the Monomoyick natives had lived here, fishing and farming in the area. In the mid 1600's, the area began to be settled by English settlers. By the 1800's there was a village on the southern end of Monomoy Island itself, but this village was eventually abandoned when the sand motion filled in the small harbor there. In 1823, the Monomoy Lighthouse was constructed at the very southern tip of Monomoy; it is still in use to assist navigation in these dangerous shoals. During World War II, the area was used for bombing practice. In 1944, the area was taken over by the U.S. Fish and Wildlife Service and became a National Wildlife Refuge.

Don't miss the Monomoy National Wildlife Refuge; it truly

is one of those "hidden gems" on Cape Cod!

Directions: Take Route 28 from Harwich to the rotary in Chatham. Then continue straight through the center of town on Main Street. After the center of town, turn right, still on Main Street, and follow this to Chatham Lighthouse on the right. After the lighthouse, bear left onto Morris Island Road and follow this past the marshes. The signs may be confusing regarding Private Property, but you can continue straight until you reach the sign to the Monomoy National Refuge. Turn left there and just up the hill to the parking area.

Google Map QR Code:

ABOUT QR CODES

QR stands for Quick Response. QR codes are similar to bar codes and were first used in 1994 in automobile manufacturing to keep track of parts for the vehicle. Now, they are used extensively for many purposes, including providing quick access to web pages.

In our book, each QR code brings you to a custom Google Map which will show you the exact location that you are looking for, as well as the other roads in the area, and where to park. The only information in the QR code is the web address of the map, nothing else; there is no tracking at all of the use of the code. The QR code simply saves having to type in a lengthy address to find the map.

You can just use your cell phone to view the QR code, and then the map will be opened quickly and easily on your phone. Once the map opens, you can zoom in to see area roads in detail; you can switch from street map view to satellite view and zoom in on the location.

If you click on a star in the map view on your phone, it will use the star as your destination and you can then use Google Maps to guide you automatically to that location using your cell phone as a free GPS. This is amazing technology, linking the printed book with our cellphones! Our book also has written directions for each location as well, including exactly how to get to each spot in the book and where to park.

Many phones now have QR code reading already built in to the camera. If your phone does not have a QR code reader already installed, you can find many apps that will read QR codes either in the Google Store or on Apple; just search for "QR Code." You also need to have the Google Maps app installed, as well as the Chrome app. Your location must be allowed in the app permission settings for both Chrome and Google maps.

FOR MORE INFORMATION

For more information about things to see on Cape Cod, check out Bill's main webpage, at ***williampeacecapecod.com*** The page has links to his other pages about bicycling on the Cape, lighthouses on Cape Cod, windmills on Cape Cod, walks and hikes on Cape Cod, playgrounds on Cape Cod, and things to do on rainy days on Cape Cod.

ABOUT THE AUTHOR

William E. Peace holds both Bachelor's and Master's degrees from Tufts University and has taught science on Cape Cod since 1973 at both the secondary and undergraduate levels. An avid nature enthusiast and bicyclist, he has lived on Cape Cod for over forty years and knows the area as only a local resident could. He has also led walks at Sandy Neck Barrier Beach, and worked as a research associate at the Cape Cod National Seashore.

The author of several books and webpages, Bill has three grown children. Besides his family, Bill is interested in photography, camping and the outdoors, computers and education, and gardening.

Bill's books include *The Cape Cod Bike Book* which was first published in 1984 and is still the go-to guide on Cape bicycling, authored by a local Cape Cod resident, and published and revised annually. He also has published a new series of *Cape Cod Visitor's Guides: Free and Inexpensive Things to Do* on the Cape, with books about the Upper Cape, Mid Cape, Lower Cape, and Outer Cape.

Each book gives a real insider's view to the Cape, information about points of interest, notes on history, ecology, where to stop, what to see, and some things that you might otherwise miss along the way. Bill loves Cape Cod, and he wants you to love it too, and he shares that passion in all of his books.

PHOTOGRAPHS

Brewster

Stony Brook Grist Mill and Herring Run: Water Wheel (p. 5), Inside the Grist Mill (p. 6), Water Sluice (p. 7), Stony Brook Grist Mill (p. 8)
Cape Cod Museum of Natural History and Hiking Trails: Museum Sign (p. 10), Wing Trail (p. 11), South Trail Observation Area (p. 12), Stony Brook Marsh (p. 13)
Drummer Boy Park & Higgins Windmill: Higgins Windmill (p. 14), Hopkins Blacksmith Shop (p.15), Gazebo at Drummer Boy Park (p. 16), Bay View from Drummer Boy Park (p. 17)
Nickerson State Park: Cape Cod Rail Trail (p. 18), Cliff Pond (p. 19), Park Road (p. 20), Nickerson Park Bike Path (p. 21)
Brewster Tidal Flats: Tidal Flats from Dunes (p. 22), Tidal Flats at Breakwater Road (p. 23), Beach and Tidal Flats (p. 25)
Punkhorn Parklands: Eagle Point Trail (p. 26), Upper Millpond from Eagle Point (p. 27), Run Pond Road (p. 28), Eagle Point Trail (p. 29)

Harwich

Bell's Neck Conservation Area: Kiosk on Bell's Neck Road (p. 30), Herring River (p. 31), Bell's Neck Road (p. 32), Herring River (p. 33)

Brook's Academy and Cranberry Bogs: Brooks Academy (p. 34), Powder House (p. 35), Brooks Park Fountain (p. 36), Harwich Cranberry Bog (p. 37)

Allen's Harbor, Wychmere Harbor and Saquatucket Harbor: Three Harbors Sign (p. 38), Allen Harbor (p. 39), Wychmere Harbor (p. 40), Saquatucket Harbor (p. 41)

Three Miles of Fun in West Harwich: Holiday Hill Ice Cream (p. 42), Holiday Hill Miniature Golf (p. 43), Harwich Go-Carts (p. 44)

Main Street, Harwich Port: Adirondack Chairs (p. 45), Bakery and Cafe (p. 46), Art Gallery (p. 47)

Playgrounds in the Lower Cape: Stony Brook Elementary School (p. 48), Eddy Elementary Play Area (p. 49), Orleans Elementary Music Area (p. 50), Brooks Park Play Area (p. 51)

Orleans

Jeremiah's Gutter: Tidal Creek (p. 52), Orleans Rotary (p. 53), View from Bridge Road (p. 54)
Rock Harbor: Harbor Pier (p. 56), Harbor Beach and Jetty (p. 57), View From Harbor (p. 59)
French Cable Museum: Cable Museum Sign (p. 60), Operator's Room (p. 61), Transatlantic Cable Roll (p. 62)
Nauset Beach: Beach Access (p. 64), Nauset Beach View (p. 65), Nauset Surfing (p. 67)
Freshwater Swimming in Orleans: Pilgrim Lake (p. 68), Pleasant Bay (p. 69)
Jonathan Young Windmill: Jonathan Young Windmill (p. 71), Tailpiece Wheel (p. 72), Town Cove View (p. 73)

Chatham

Chatham Fish Pier: Chatham Fish Market (p. 74), Boat at Pier (p. 75)

Chatham Railroad Museum: Railroad Museum Entrance (p. 77), Red Caboose (p. 78), Ticket Window (p. 79)

Benjamin Godfrey Windmill and Chase Park: Godfrey Windmill (p. 80), Chase Park (p. 82), Chase Park Labyrinth (p. 83)

Chatham Lighthouse: Chatham Lighthouse (p. 84), Chatham Lighthouse (p. 85), Coast Guard Boat (p. 86), Coast Guard Sign (p. 87)

Main Street, Chatham: Five and Ten (p. 88), Theater (p. 89), Main Street View (p. 90), Candy Store (p. 91)

Monomoy National Wildlife Refuge: Visitor Center (p. 92), Stairs to Beach (p. 93), Upper Air Work Area and Dome (p. 94), Fishing At Monomoy (p. 96)

INDEX

Brewster

Harwich

Orleans

Chatham

Notes

Printed in Great Britain
by Amazon

35258812R00061